Igor Lebedev
Alexander Kuznetsov

The study of the lower layers of the psyche

Igor Lebedev
Alexander Kuznetsov

The study of the lower layers of the psyche

as a basis for special psychological research on the PsyScanner

ScienciaScripts

This book is a translation from the original published under ISBN 978-620-4-20064-4.

Publisher:
Sciencia Scripts
is a trademark of
Dodo Books Indian Ocean Ltd. and OmniScriptum S.R.L publishing group

120 High Road, East Finchley, London, N2 9ED, United Kingdom
Str. Armeneasca 28/1, office 1, Chisinau MD-2012, Republic of Moldova, Europe
Managing Directors: Ieva Konstantinova, Victoria Ursu
info@omniscriptum.com

Printed at: see last page
ISBN: 978-620-4-04853-6

Kuznetsov Alexander Yuryevich Director General of the Center for Information and Psychological Security **Lebedev Igor Borisovich** Doctor of Psychological Sciences, Professor

PsyScanner is an innovative tool of non-local holographic resonance, the results of its practical use as a base for special psychological research in the study of the lower layers of the psyche.

Table of contents

Contents with abstract

Introduction: In the introduction the relevance of PsyScanner and the method of nonlocal holographic resonance in the study of lower layers of psyche: nonlocal (unconscious) and "pralogical" (mystical) thinking is considered. The object, subject, goals and tasks of the research are disclosed. The hypothesis of research is disclosed.

The object of the study is the human psyche as a whole,

representing several different levels.

Subject of research: two initial levels of human mental development in phylogeny: the preconscious level of mental development ("unconscious"),

level of "primitive thinking" of modern man, better known as mystical thinking and its practical embodiment - magic.

Purpose of the research: studying and diagnosing the lower layers of mental development while carrying out special research on the PsyScanner APC.

Research objectives: to describe the method of non-local holographic resonance and the results of its practical use with the use of "PsyScanner". To consider basic levels of development of human mentality in ontogenesis and phylogeny.

Research hypothesis: Studying and cognizing work of the human brain it becomes more and more clear that it is such a complex mechanism, that it is beyond our power to understand it. Theory of non-local holographic resonance, based on basic postulates of quantum physics, will allow to solve a part of tasks, connected with study of our psyche. The theory of non-local holographic resonance contrasts principles of quantum physics and Young's synchronism with the fundamental physical principle of causality and describes synchronism as a constantly acting in nature creative principle, ordering events in a "non-physical" (non-causal) way, only based on their meaning related to any "non-physical" (non-obvious) interrelation of events regardless of their separation in time and space.

Chapter 1 The chapter discusses the stages of mental development in phylogeny.

Abstract: In order to understand the role of magical consciousness in life of modern man it is important for us to understand the general dynamic structure of our psyche. The most ancient structure of consciousness is magical thinking, this stage is called primitive thinking (or pralogical) As sign culture was mastered in phylogenesis man became human-minded (homo sapiens) and this means that he developed consciousness. Consequently, *consciousness is a special form of reflection of the surrounding world that is peculiar only to humans.* Thus, preconscious and sign (semiotic) levels of mental reflection constitute the basic layers of the psyche and influence the whole life of a human, determining in many respects his behavior.

Chapter 2 The psyche as a non-local reality of our world

Abstract: The world we live in consists of two realities: material and mental. Since Plato's time, philosophers have argued: what is primary is matter or idea. Therefore, it is better to understand matter as corpuscularly concentrated energy (however, science does not know what kind of reality was initially "concentrated"). By psyche we usually mean the ability of living beings (not all, but only those with a developed nervous system) to reflect matter in the form of a mental image. These two realities coexist together in living organisms, such as humans. The chapter reveals the difference between these two realities

Chapter 3 Nelocality as a basic principle of mental functioning.

Abstract: The chapter deals with thinking as a stage of development and the basis of magical thinking. The material world in the framework of "human dimensionality" is endowed with signs of locality, it is placed in the space-time continuum, from which it is inseparable. If we "go down" to the level of atoms and subatomic particles, we will find, as quantum physics teaches us, that so familiar to us characteristics of reality are strongly violated.

The widely known principle of "quantum entanglement" suggests that in the material world as well, in some cases there is a violation of locality and objects begin to interact with each other coherently, although they are not connected by any forces. Also objects break the postulate about rigid locality of the material world.

Our approach boils down to the fact that locality is a small and temporary island in the boundless ocean of nonlocality and that our psyche is one of the manifestations of nonlocality. Recognizing in psychology the existence of the principle of nonlocality as a system-forming concept, we would be able to explain a huge range of parapsychic phenomena, which today's classical psychology tries not to notice.

The nonlocality hypothesis found its confirmation in theory and practice of holography. Integral, volumetric image of objects was received not from "folding" of primary elements, but actually was manifested from emptiness. A holographic plate could be broken on the smallest parts and thus each splinter kept a total quantity of information about the original, but in this case the quality of image worsened. In this way every point on the holographic plate carries a complete set of information about the original and every point on the original is reflected in every point of the plate.

In the history of mankind appearances of deities, saints, etc., that took place in crowds of people (for example, the "Fatima miracle") were nothing else but a demonstration of a three-dimensional spatial hologram to the audience.

Mental reflection most of all resembles a hologram, but unlike a laser hologram, a "living" hologram, with which a medium of a psyche can perform any manipulations at will.

Chapter 4 Primitive thinking as a stage of mental development and the basis of magical thinking.

Abstract: "Primitive thinking" is the thinking inherent in primitive peoples, those peoples who resemble by their organization the social order of the Stone Age. The famous researcher of primitive thinking in primitive peoples was Lucien Levy-Bruhl. Primitive thinking covers a long stage of formation (the period from the sympractical stage of language existence and approximately up to the appearance of written language). At the stage of primitive thinking the origin and development of modern language as a sign-mediated system of reflection took place.

Communication with the outside world was established by certain people in the tribe, with the help of special rituals. Ritual was not criticized in any way. It was all an effort to explain the world. The "image of the world" had not changed for centuries. The progress of primitive thinking of ancient man was imperceptible for thousands of years.

Unlike modern man, primitive man pays attention to the subjective, mystical world, where everything depends on the influence of spirit forces on people and on each other. We, on the other hand, pay attention to the objective world, the real world.

There are two basic principles in primitive, aka magical, thinking. The first is that like produces like; or the cause is like the effect. The second is that things that have interacted with each other at least once continue this interaction even after the termination of direct contact. In general, for a simpler designation, the first principle can be called the "law of similarity", and the second - the "law of contagion".

There are two more views of the world, from the side of magic. Imitative - based on the principle of likeness. Contagious - based on the principle of contagion.

Possessors of primitive thinking - primitive people - never subjected to the analysis of the meaningful side of their magical actions, but knew only practical. In representatives of primitive thinking, there is no distinction between received information during a dream or in reality.

What all primitive peoples have in common is that a magical rather than causal connection of events and phenomena is recognized as real.

The language of "primitive thinking" is interesting. One of the distinguishing characteristics of primitive language is its amazing detail and precision in marking objects, situations and actions.

Sign language is of great importance among ancient peoples. It is very and very rich, actively used by hunters on the hunt, by women during mourning, by witches and herbalists for secret negotiations.

The modern man is more mystical than it is considered to be, than we admit it to ourselves. "Periphery" of our consciousness, which is a very significant part of it, is filled with semantic fields carrying information of "primitive thinking".

One form of representation in the consciousness of "primitive thinking" is dreams. "Primitive thinking" is a sign, but dologic (pralogic according to Levi-Brühl) form of reflection of the surrounding world, therefore more intrinsic to science than to art. Mysticism and magic are based on the principles of "primitive thinking".

Chapter 5 The manifestation of mystical thinking (magical) in human dreams.

Abstract: The chapter deals with "primitive thinking" - this thinking is inherent to primitive peoples, those peoples who resemble by their organization the social order of the Stone Age. The famous researcher of primitive thinking in primitive peoples was Lucien Levy-Bruhl. Primitive thinking covers a long stage of formation (the period from the sympractical stage of language existence and approximately up to the appearance of written language). At the stage of primitive thinking the origin and development of modern language as a sign-mediated system of reflection took place.

Communication with the outside world was established by certain people in the tribe, with the help of special rituals. The ritual was not criticized in any way.

Unlike modern man, primitive man pays attention to the subjective, mystical world, where everything depends on the influence of spirit forces on people and on each other. We, on the other hand, pay attention to the objective world, the real world.

There are two basic principles in primitive, aka magical, thinking. The first is that like produces like; or the cause is like the effect. The second is that things that have interacted with each other at least once continue this interaction even after direct contact ceases. In general, for a simpler designation, the first principle can be called the "law of similarity", and the second - the "law of contagion".

There are two more views of the world, from the side of magic. Imitative - based on the principle of likeness. Contagious - based on the principle of contagion.

Possessors of primitive thinking - primitive people - never subjected to the analysis of the meaningful side of their magical actions, but knew only practical. In representatives of primitive thinking, there is no distinction between received information during a dream or in reality.

What all primitive peoples have in common is that a magical rather than causal connection of events and phenomena is recognized as real.

The language of "primitive thinking" is interesting. One of the distinguishing characteristics of primitive language is its amazing detail and precision in marking objects, situations and actions.

Sign language is of great importance among ancient peoples. It is very and very rich, actively used by hunters on the hunt, by women during mourning, by witches and herbalists for secret negotiations.

The modern man is more mystical than it is considered to be, than we admit it to ourselves. "Periphery" of our consciousness, which is a very significant part of it, is filled with semantic fields carrying information of "primitive thinking".

One form of representation in the consciousness of "primitive thinking" is dreams. "Primitive thinking" is a sign, but dologic (pralogic according to Levi-Brühl) form of reflection of the surrounding world, therefore more intrinsic to science than to art. Mysticism and magic are based on the principles of "primitive thinking".

Chapter 6Basic   principles of the brain to activate its own resources in terms of quantum physics and psychophysiology

The chapter discusses the basic principles of how the brain works to activate its own resources in terms of quantum physics and psychophysiology.

The more we learn about the brain, the more it becomes clear that it is such a complex mechanism that we cannot understand it. One could argue that there is nothing more complex in the whole universe than the human brain and how it works. Pavlov and these kinds of scientists see the brain as some kind of mechanism, but they have not been able to prove it, nor can the percentage composition of the brain tell us anything about how this incredible organism functions.

If we do an experiment to determine the timing of decision making, maybe using evoked potentials, then the brain will show that it made a decision before you even pressed a button or did something like that. The work of the limbic system, which is involved in the regulation of internal organ functions, automatic regulation, emotions, memory, sleep, wakefulness, etc., is reviewed. **The basic principles of how the brain works to activate its own resources are reviewed**

Each brain is unique because it has a neural network written on it, a given personality, a given life with all the individual associations, what you listened to, what you ate, what you saw. The brain develops all the time, if effort is made it develops faster than if we make no effort at all.

Modern psychological tests and polygraph tests are very time consuming and require high professionalism of an employee who conducts them. The results are often directly dependent on the experience and subjective qualities of the specialist, rather than the personal qualities of the tested person. That is why PsyScanner was created

The principle of PsyScanner is based on non-local holographic resonance which allows identifying even the smallest changes in the semantic state of a person, i.e. is able to catch the slightest changes in the physical and psychological state of a person.

The main advantages of PsyScanner are the rapid, comprehensive examination via the Internet, as well as a detailed diagnosis report on the symptoms of psychosomatic illnesses.

Chapter 7The method of nonlocal holographic resonance and results of its practical application

Chapter 6 discusses the non-local holographic resonance method and the results of its practical application.

The method of nonlocal holographic resonance allows not only to obtain objective information about the psychophysiological state, but also to carry out nonlocal psychocorrection, which allows to carry out recruitment and placement more effectively and provide neutralization of intrapersonal factors of failure and resource disclosure [9].

The principle of non-local holographic resonance method is the following: if some semiotic nano-information is "recorded" on a computer and then presented in a very short time, then psyche of an athlete reacts to such presentation by building a full image. Thus, the use of the method of non-local holographic resonance gives an opportunity to study human psyche, as well as to carry out psychocorrective influence

The devices in question have already been created, have been tested in practice, and have positive results and reviews. The method of psychodiagnostics and psychocorrection is called "nonlocal holographic resonance system", and the devices themselves are called "PsyScanner" holographic psychodiagnostic device and "Encoder" holographic psychocorrection device. All instruments of nonlocal

holographic resonance have undergone many years (more than ten years), approbation and verification. The main advantages of these tools created on the basis of non-local holographic resonance are high reliability, ease of use, easy interpretation of the results and very high performance - in 15-20   minutes the test taker answers 2,000 to 2,500 questions.

Thus, we can assert that the principle of holographic nature of human mentality has passed from the theoretical to the practical plane.

Introduction

Relevance of PsyScanner and non-local holographic resonance method for studying lower layers of psyche: non-local (unconscious) and "pralogical" (mystical) thinking

The psyche of a modern man consists of several conditional levels, which we call unconscious (pre-conscious); the level of 'primitive thinking' inherited from the stage of primitive communal formation and formed during ontogenesis. It is the level of primitive thinking that is the aim of the present study because magical thinking appears there; then, chronologically, a layer of formal-logical thinking appears, a variant of which is "imperative thinking". The emergence of "imperative thinking" fell on an important stage in the development of mankind that was connected with the transition from the stage of "collecting" to that of "productivity". Finally, the last, the uppermost level of consciousness is the so-called systemic-scientific thinking that started to form already in the era of pre-classical science and got an especially powerful impulse in its development in the Cartesianism era (from the 17th century up to the present day). Among these levels two have a special representation in the life of modern man: it is the level of "mystical thinking",

manifested in the form of "magical thinking" (we understand the relationship between mysticism and magic as theory and practice). And the level of formal-logical thinking, often manifested in the organization of human behavior, as imperative thinking. Modern man, is no less mystical than his distant ancestor, although there is a lot of logic and science in his life.

Object of study.

The object of research in our work is the human psyche as a whole, which represents several different levels. These levels were formed in phylogenesis, but are also actively manifested in the ontogenetic development of each person's psyche.

Subject of the study.

The two initial levels of human mental development in phylogeny are the subject of the study:

1. The preconscious level of mental development, often referred to as the "unconscious";

2. level of "primitive thinking" of modern man, more known as mystical thinking and its practical embodiment - magic. **Objective of the research.**

Studying and diagnosing the lower layers of mental development during special studies on the PsyScanner APC.

Research Objectives.

1. To consider the main levels of human mental development in ontogeny and phylogeny.

2. To consider the level of "primitive thinking" consciousness as the main supplier of mystical-magical representations.

3. The manifestation of magical thinking in the visions of modern

a man.

4. Describe the basic principles of mental work to activate

own resources in terms of quantum physics and psychophysiology.

5. To describe the method of non-local holographic resonance and the results of its practical use with the use of the "PsyScanner" APC

Research Hypothesis.

According to scientific

psychological research, the psyche

of the modern individual consists of several levels. One of the most basic cognitive levels of the psyche is the one formed back in

phylogeny is the level of "mystical thinking". The level of mystical thinking appeared in Cro-Magnon man during the origin of consciousness, i.e. the sign system of reflection. According to the most conservative anthropological calculations, this period began 50-100 thousand years ago and continues to this day. At the level of "primitive thinking" the laws of information processing are in force. Such as: contagiosity, partisanship, etc. For a long time up to the appearance of formal-logical thinking (about 10-12 thousand years ago) "primitive thinking" was the only way of mankind to realize the world around us. In ontogenetic development, psyche repeats all levels of consciousness development. That is, **mysticomagic ways of information processing are actively inherent in modern man as well, though he does not always guess about it.**

By studying and learning the workings of the human brain, it becomes more and more clear that it is such a complex mechanism that it is beyond our comprehension. It can be argued that there is nothing more complex in the universe than the human brain and how it works. It could be argued that of all that we know, nothing can be compared with the human brain.

The theory of non-local holographic resonance based on basic postulates of quantum physics, in particular the phenomenon of "quantum entanglement" as well as fundamental theoretical statements of C.G. Jung about the collective unconscious and the phenomenon, designated by Jung as synchronism, on the concept of anticipation created by the Russian psychologist B.F. Lomov, corresponding member of the USSR Academy of Sciences, and the results of experimental research, which were obtained in the laboratory of Professor V.N. Pushkin will allow to solve some problems, connected with In the theory of non-local holographic resonance the principles of quantum physics and Young's synchronism are opposed to the fundamental physical principle of causality and describe synchronism as a constantly acting in nature creative principle that ordering events in a "non-physical" (non-causal) way, only on the basis of their meaning related to any "non-physical" (non-obvious) interrelation of events regardless of their separation in time and space.

Chapter 1

Stages of mental development in phylogeny.

The first attempt to scientifically answer the questions of **what our psyche and consciousness is all about** dates back to the late 19th century, to the studies of the founder of experimental psychology W. Wundt.

It is true that **Wundt divided** the possibility of studying the psyche and consciousness in his research **into two constituent parts. The first part is the lower mental functions.** To them Wundt referred: **sensation, perception, attention**. He believed that this part of the psyche and consciousness is quite **possible to study experimentally**. Recall that Wundt's experiment is not a purely nomothetic experiment of Cartesian science. Wundt's experiment is half-hearted; on the one hand it is introspective, and on the other it has all the characteristics of a scientific experiment. Wundt's method was called - introspective experiment. It is important for us to understand this because Wundt's conception of the structure of human consciousness depended directly on the empirical possibilities of his method. Wundt believed that only lower mental functions could be investigated empirically. Therefore, Wundt could not investigate thinking, memory, speech, i.e., everything that forms the basis of consciousness, by experience and turned to mythology, ethnography, and cultural history for this purpose. Thus, Wundt left the possibility of investigating higher forms of consciousness to the humanities. Hence, in the early 20th century, it was the representative of ethnography and cultural studies who had the honor of investigating the most ancient structures of consciousness - magical thinking. [3]

Let us note another important aspect of Wundt's research, namely: Wundt was a proponent of English empiricism and his ideas about consciousness fell within the famous formula of empiricists: "consciousness is the sum of sensations". Thus, in the study of the psyche, Wundt took the "conscious path", ruling out the presence of any unconscious in the structure of the psyche. At about the same time, in the mid-19th century, Western philosophy (Schopenhauer, Nietzsche, Kierkegaard, Hartmann, Herbar, etc.) was actively developing the concept of the unconscious. And at the beginning of the 20th century, Freud practically absolutized the category of the unconscious, placing it at the head of all mental development. Freud's unconsciousness was endowed with all signs of mythologized consciousness (though, by the way, Freud managed to treat magic negatively).

In order to **understand the role of magical consciousness in life of modern man, it is important for us to understand the general dynamic structure of our psyche**. Human consciousness (as Cro-Magnon man), as a reasonable man, began to develop as the first people mastered a sign system of reflection. At the end of the 20th century, the cultural-historical approach to explaining people's psyche and behavior developed by the Soviet psychologist L.S. Vygotsky began to spread in our country.

Vygotsky's concept assumed a special role in the development of psyche and consciousness of the cultural historical environment that surrounded and changed a person. The leading place in this formation of consciousness, according to L.S. Vygotsky, belonged to signs as conditional ideal substitutes for real things and objects of the material world [4]. **As sign culture was mastered in phylogenesis, man became human-intelligent (homo sapiens), which means that he developed consciousness**. Consequently, *consciousness is a **special form of reflection of the surrounding world that is peculiar only to man**. It is not accidental that the root word "consciousness" is a word "sign"*. Just as a fire, when bursting out, lights up the whole big part of space, so consciousness, when developing, covers the whole big part of mentality. **The problem of the unconscious, outside the problem of consciousness does not exist. The conscious and the unconscious are elements of a single system, the name of which is the human psyche**. The ratio of conscious and unconscious is the ratio of sign (mediated) and extra sign (direct) reflection in psyche. We can say that there is no problem of the unconscious, as such, but there is a problem of correlation of different levels of reflection (sign and non-sign) among themselves. Certain stages are distinguished in the development of sign reflection, as well as in the development of the psyche as a whole in phylogeny. First, the stage of precognitive development of the psyche. Every person is born with mentality, mentality is given to us from birth, the formation of mentality in the first months of child's life leads to the beginning of sign reflection, that is, to the origin of consciousness. Scientific researches show that if in this period a child does not begin to master sign-reflection (i.e. he remains a "Mowgli"), it will be almost impossible in the following years; a man will become feral.

As the sign culture is mastered, man enters the second stage of development of his own psyche. As French ethnographer Lucien Levy-Brühl said - this stage is called primitive thinking (or pralogical thinking) [7].

After the formation of primitive thinking, a powerful change occurs in the historical development of mankind: man turns from a "gatherer" to a "producer". This transition takes place about 12,000 years ago. It is quite possible that the reason for such transformation was a certain mythologized phenomenon, which received the well-known name of the "world flood" in cultural studies. Some force or circumstance, of which we can only speculate, forced humanity to leave its traditional habitat, to gather in vast communities, which later became city-states or even the first State on Earth (the Sumerian Kingdom), and to begin to grow cereals and domesticate livestock. **This led not only to the division of labour, but also to the development of the sciences, on the human psyche, it was "imprinted" in the form of**
the emergence of a new layer of consciousness that we conventionally call imperative thinking, when the processing of sign information began to be carried out not according to the laws of primitive thinking, i.e. magic, but taking into account the laws of logic   (Aristotle)   [1]:

The law of identity, the law (prohibition) of contradiction, the law of the excluded third. At this stage, not only the sciences developed, the logic of thinking was formed, but there was also the formation of what is now called folk wisdom. Folk wisdom was accumulated in special linguistic formations: proverbs, fables, phraseology, proverbs, winged words, etc. Folk wisdom is always a kind of instructions, teachings, how to act or not to act. It is a certain vector of behavior, that is - a certain imperative (rule, which should be followed). Here I would like to notice that the magical thinking and the conventional wisdom are absolutely different concepts that designate different stages of the consciousness development. The 3rd stage of psychical development in phylogenesis was followed by the 4th stage, the so-called **"system thinking". The 4th stage** [9] started developing during the period of the first sciences originating. The peak of its development was the 17th century, the epoch of Cartesianism conception.

Thus, precognitive and sign (semiotic) levels of mental reflection constitute the basic layers of the psyche and influence the whole life of a person, determining in many respects his behavior.

Chapter 2

The psyche as a non-local reality of our world

Everyone knows from experience that the world in which we live consists of two realities: material and mental. Since Plato's times, philosophers have argued: what is primary is matter or idea. But we are interested in this dispute from quite different positions. Matter is reality, perceived by us in the process of psychical reflection. Here it is necessary to mention that not all matter is perceived by a man in the form of psychical reflection. For example, we do not see practically the whole basic spectrum of force interactions: gravitational, strong and weak interactions, electromagnetic (except for light).

Therefore, by matter, it is better to mean corpuscularly concentrated energy (at the same time, what kind of reality was initially "concentrated" is unknown to science).

By psyche we usually mean the ability of living beings (not all, but only those with a developed nervous system) to reflect matter in the form of a mental image.

These two realities in living organisms, such as humans, coexist together. How do these two realities differ from each other? In principle, they differ in that one reality, the psyche, is completely nonlocal. To understand the nonlocality of the psyche, let us first consider matter as a localized reality. Let us first note some organic characteristics of matter. It exists in a space-time continuum, in which it can have up to four dimensions: length, width, height and a monodirectional vector of time.

Further, matter, namely one of its forms - substance, has the property to be in a certain place of space, i.e. to be localized in the coordinate system, similarly as in time. As a consequence of localization the property of matter - motion, i.e.

moving from one localization to another, appears. Matter possesses mass, i.e. the ability to concentrate matter in a certain quantity in a certain place. The motion of matter is always carried out with a given velocity, the value of which cannot exceed the speed of propagation of electromagnetic waves in vacuum.

As Einstein suggested, matter and energy are equivalent. The proton, which is the quintessence of matter, in fact, is a clot of quark-gluon plasma, which at decay turns into energy.

So, matter is energy localized in space and time, possessing a limited speed of movement and obeying certain rules or laws.

A completely different picture emerges in the analysis of psyche. The psyche is not just an ability to reflect in the form of an image, it is also an ability to perform certain actions with this image, for example: to reduce to a point, to expand to the size of the universe, to move from one place to any other, with movement speed being almost instantaneous. Apart from spatial manipulations any temporal changes are also possible: the time vector can be directed in any direction, as well as stopped. Today it becomes clear that the psyche is a reality, in which such basic characteristics of the material world as space, time, motion, energy are completely absent. And all other laws of nature also lose all meaning. Everything that happens in the psyche is mainly subordinate to the carrier's will only. Also, unlike matter, which is subordinate to the local principle, everything that happens in the psyche is absolutely non-local.

Chapter 3

Non-locality as a basic principle of mental functioning.

Let us consider what locality and non-locality are in relation to the world in which we exist.

The material world, in the framework of "human dimensionality", i.e. not in cosmology and not in quantum physics, is endowed with signs of locality, it is placed in a space-time continuum, from which it is inseparable.

If we "go down" to the level of atoms and subatomic particles, we find, as quantum physics teaches us, that, so familiar to us, characteristics of reality are strongly disturbed.

The widely known principle of "quantum entanglement" suggests that in the material world as well, in some cases there is a violation of locality and objects begin to interact with each other coherently, although they are not connected by any forces. Also objects break the postulate about rigid locality of the material world.

However, in general, in the dimensions of the world in which man exists, nature has found a certain balance, special and subtle, which allows subordinating this world to mathematically verified laws.

Our approach boils down to the fact that locality is a small and temporary island in the boundless ocean of nonlocality and that one of the manifestations of nonlocality is our psyche. Nevertheless, nonlocality, "breaking in" periodically into the local world of our perceptions, is the mother of all physical and mental mysteries. Recognizing in psychology the existence of the principle of nonlocality as a system-forming concept, we could explain a huge range of parapsychic phenomena, which today's classical psychology tries not to notice.

One of the defenders of locality in classical physics was Albert Einstein. As early as 1936, he wrote that "the most incomprehensible in this world is its comprehensibility. Einstein believed that the known laws of the world exist because of its locality. In a sense, the scientist was right: locality makes our world understandable to ourselves. Locality allows us to have the science that we have. Thus, it can be stated that nature within "common sense" is local. This is quite different in the reality of the psychic.

In the material world, locality is necessary for our own good. The term locality itself appeared in the 17th century literally in English means "locality", and in scientific and philosophical context, that everything has its own place. We can always point to a material object and determine its place in this or that system of coordinates. Locality is the basis of order, which points us not only to an object's place, but also to its relations and connections with other objects. Locality thus highlights in any arrangement of objects a certain hierarchy and system. Systemicity is impossible in a nonlocal world; the second law of thermodynamics is, precisely, the law of transition from locality to nonlocality as applied to "closed" material objects. Everything in nature tends to go beyond the rigid boundaries of locality and return not to chaos, but to the primordial state of nonlocality.

On the contrary, psyche is non-local, it is impossible to single out a primary element in it (what the founder of classical experimental psychology Wilhelm Wundt tried to do unsuccessfully), therefore all attempts to systematize the world of mental phenomena are unsuccessful up to now. A mental image is a hologram, while a hologram disappears at an attempt to transfer it from a volume into a plane.

Ancient Greek philosophers of the pre-Platonic period argued mainly about whether the world is stable or dialectical, whether it obeys laws or whether, as Heraclitus wrote, "everything flows, everything changes". The locality of the world allowed us to retain hope of being able to understand and cognize the world, while nonlocality discouraged us. This was always the case until quantum mechanics came along. That's why one of the founders of quantum theory, Albert Einstein, fought so hard afterwards against the principle of non-locality in the construction of matter. Einstein saw non-locality as a ghostly action at a distance, something akin to magic and it was frightening. He thought it was a return to scholasticism, to the notion of ether, of which he was the theoretical gravedigger. Einstein believed that the world is in fact local and only appears non-local and that one must simply find a more adequate theory "correctly" explaining all the "quirks" of quantum physics. Further development of science settled the argument of great physics theorists A. Einstein and N. Bohr: the world really conceals nonlocality at all levels.

There is a great non-local revolution in modern science, no matter who or how one wants it. At the same time, in psychological science today, meaning primarily classical psychology, there is only one type of explanation of behavior - it is locality, highlighting a chain of mechanisms, determinisms of behavior, which spread continuously through space, from one point to another, gradually, step-by-step.

Naturally, classical science "clings" to local explanations, for it is localism that has brought science the success it has had over the last 400 years of Cartesianism.

In science, the ability to predict human behavior based on mathematical equations, the principles of reliability, validity, and accuracy is highly valued. Who and why do we need a science in which uncertainty and indeterminism exist instead of accurate foresight, in which it is impossible to systematize and describe.

Initially, the nonlocality hypothesis found its confirmation in theory and practice of holography. Integral, volumetric image of objects was obtained not from "folding" of primary elements, but actually manifested from emptiness. Using a special laser shooting method, a photoplate with stripes and spots which have nothing in common with the original was firstly produced. Then such a plate was put under the split laser beam again and then the volumetric image of the object appeared in the air, which was perceived from any point of view, that is, unlike the photo, one could bypass it from all sides and see all its details. But the most interesting thing was that it was possible to break the holographic plate into the smallest parts and thus each shard kept the total amount of information about the original, but in this case the quality of image worsened. Thus every point on the holographic plate carries the full set of information about the original and every point on the original is reflected in every point of the plate. It is this way of capturing information about an object that best illustrates the principle of locality in our commensurability. Physicists have suggested that a hologram of an object is a standing light wave. Some quantum physicists (David Bohm) have allowed the possibility of extending the holographic principle to the field of macroobjects of the Universe: i.e. stars, planets, galaxies and everything, everything, everything in the Universe is a standing wave similar to an optical hologram.

Here it's appropriate to remember that phenomena of deities, saints, etc., which took place in crowds of people (for example, Fatima miracle) were nothing else but demonstration of three-dimensional spatial hologram for spectators in the history of mankind.

In principle, Plato was probably the first ancient scholar to describe exactly such a structure of the world (an idea is an image, a hologram of a material object).

The model of the world, according to Plato, turns out to be acceptable if we assume that the whole Universe has the form of "Hypersphere" and that every object in it is a standing wave located simultaneously in all points of the Universe.

Such assumption has a deep worldview meaning. For if all objects are in a wave form hidden from an observer and can be perceived in any point of the Universe, then many phenomena of parapsychology are explainable. The main condition: "to provide in the given point of space necessary focusing" (V.N. Pushkin), in other words, it is necessary to enter **non-local mental resonance**, which would allow an observer to find hidden in each point wave structures of objects, being on considerable distance from the observer.

Mental reflection most of all resembles a hologram, but unlike a laser hologram, a "living" hologram, with which a medium of a psyche can perform any manipulations at will.

And the most important question of modern worldview. Does psychic reality exist outside a material medium, and if so, where does it exist, where is its home?

It is thought that understanding of psyche as non-local reality will help mankind to find right answers on mysteries of the Universe.

Chapter 4

Primitive thinking as a stage of mental development and the basis of magical thinking.

"Primitive thinking" is the thinking inherent in primitive peoples, "natural peoples," as they are often called by Western researchers. These are those peoples who resemble by their organization the social order of the Stone Age.

A famous researcher of primitive thinking in primitive peoples was Lucien Levy-Bruhl. Primitive thinking covers a long stage of formation (the period from the sympractical stage of language existence and approximately up to the appearance of written language). Actually, the origin and development of modern language as a sign-mediated system of reflection took place at the stage of primitive thinking. The type of organization of man's orientation and research activity on constructing the "image of the world" and the image of reality surrounding him at this stage had its own peculiarities and differed greatly from the thinking of the modern man. The first fundamental difference of primitive thinking from ours is its so-called pragmatic or mystic character. At the same time one should not at all understand illogical as illogical. The primitive people are not alien to logic in general; where it is a question of concrete behaviour: hunting, agriculture, fishing, war with another tribe, the primitive man acts logically, but without thinking over this process, without giving excessive theoretical meaning to such his actions [7]. But where an attempt is made to go beyond specific behaviour and to explain, for instance, why hunting was successful yesterday and not today, primitive man becomes alien in logic and seeks an explanation of the cause of his actions in mysticism [7]. Mystical reasons occupy the entire theoretical space of primitive man's consciousness. Primitive thinking, for instance, admits that the same being can be in two or more places at the same time. It is subject to the law of complicity (participation) and is totally indifferent to contradictions which our mind does not tolerate. If the collective beliefs of a tribe assert that the ancestor of the tribe is the sun, some animal or a boulder by the river, everyone sincerely believes that this is indeed the case, that the whole tribe is a partaker of this object. The contribution of Levy-Bruhl is that he was the first to challenge the theory of animalism, which held that man was originally given a single type of thinking. Levy-Bruhl believed that the types of thinking of different historical periods are different. At the same time, modern man is characterized not only by modern types of thinking. Each of us, at the periphery of our consciousness, is a bearer of rudiments of past types of thinking. Long before Jung, Levi-Brühl guessed and spoke about so-called "collective representations" of ancient people, transmitted through the unconscious. Rites of initiation (initiation), other obligatory rituals in which the stories of myths and fairy tales are re-played, serve to pass them on to younger group members. The strongest emotional background often overshadows the cognitive component. Everything in the world for the primitive man has some mystical power. The information received both while awake and asleep is equally real.

The fact that primitive people practically never improved anything is also striking. Labor tools, which are difficult to manufacture, remain unchanged and unmodified for many centuries [7].

And here it is a matter of ideology, in belief in mystical properties of objects connected with their external component, and not in the fact that primitive people had conservative thinking. If they changed the external component of an object - its form, in their opinion, it could lead to violation of interaction of this object with the environment. Innovation was strictly punishable. And people rather preferred to sacrifice the innovator so that he would not endanger the whole tribe.

Communication with the outside world was established by certain people in the tribe, with the help of special rituals. The ritual was not criticized in any way. If suddenly nothing happened after dancing around the fire, it was not the ritual that was not actually doing anything, but the people who created the wrong conditions - wrong dancing, bringing bad branches, bad singing - who were to blame. All of this was an effort to explain the world. "The image of the world" had not changed for centuries. The progress of primitive thinking of ancient man has been imperceptible for millennia.

So, unlike modern man, primitive man sees everything differently. The primitive pays attention to the subjective, mystical world, where everything depends on the influence of the forces of spirits on people and on each other. We, on the other hand, pay attention to the objective, real world.

Now let's go deeper into the subject of primitive thinking. There are **two main principles** in primitive, aka magical, thinking. The first one is that **the like produces the like**; or the cause is like the effect. The second is that **things, which at least once interacted with each other, continue this interaction even after direct contact ceases**. In general, for a simpler designation, **the first principle may be called the "law of likeness" and the second, the "law of contagion".** A shaman, a priest, a magician, with respect to the first principle, can conclude that he is able to produce any desired action by simply imitating it. And from the second one, that any action taken in relation to a certain object will also reflect on the person who has ever interacted with it.

There are two more views of the world, from the side of magic. Imitative - based on the principle of likeness. Contagious - based on the principle of contagion.

For tens of thousands of years, these two views determined a meaningful side of the worldview of primitive/ancient people. Possessors of primitive thinking - primitive people - never subjected to the analysis of the substantial side of their magical actions, but knew only practical.

One example of witchcraft incorporating the principles of imitative and contagious magic is a doll. From an intended victim, hair, nails, eyelashes, and saliva are taken, and then by means of wax, a doll is created, which is slowly burned for 7 days.

But it is worth noting that magic, in primitive thinking, is represented not only as an evil force, but is also used for good. In ancient Greece, for example, if a person was mistakenly thought to be dead and while he was not, or he was not found, funeral rites were performed on him, he was still considered dead until the rite of a new birth. And only after the rite was carefully performed, the person would again enter into communion with other people.

Representatives of primitive thinking have no distinction between the information received in a dream or in reality. If a person received information in a dream, it means that some spirit has brought it to him, which means that the information is as reliable as if he received it in a waking state.

It is not so important, for ancient people, that the ritual does not work. The important thing was that it was done, and most importantly, that it was done right. A man might die, in the primitive viewpoint, not from a blow with a spear but because an enemy had visited on him evil spirits, and they took his life by possessing the same spear. In primitive man, the antecedent is often confused and confused with the cause of the event. Primitive man's thinking is not only primitive but also at times paradoxical. Sometimes the opposite happens: in the most immediate and obvious way related phenomena are not associated in the mind of primitive man. For example, if a person was bitten by a snake, then death came not because of a snake bite, but because of the induced spoilage. This is the way the primitive thinking of the ancient man is arranged.

What all primitive peoples have in common is that a magical rather than causal connection of events and phenomena is recognised as real. Even the seasons change only thanks to sacred rituals. The concept of the soul, which originated in the epoch of "imperative thinking" (religion), is not inherent in primitive man.

The primitive man feels his mystical unity with all living and inanimate matter surrounding him. [7]

The law of participation (partaking) complements our notions of primitive consciousness. The Indian, by putting the feathers of an eagle on his head, pursues not only the purpose of decorating himself: he trades in the sight, foresight, strength and wisdom of the bird with the feathers. The complicity underlying the collective representation is what makes him act in this way.

The law of contradiction operates in all mental operations: in collective representations and individual mental life, since there is no clear boundary between the social and the individual at all. However, there are operations in which the law of contradiction cannot be dispensed with. The logical and the pralogical exist in the same consciousness together, closely interrelated. For all this, the mental process on which the main intellectual work falls is memory. The primitive man must constantly use a huge number of the most complex collective representations with the whole complex of details, in a strictly defined sequence - it is necessary for carrying out any action, guiding it.

It is necessary to remember rites, rituals, incantations, as well as a huge number of practical signs: traces, smells, sounds, topographical information, skills. All necessary knowledge is transmitted verbally from generation to generation, there is no written language as such yet, so memory is the most important mechanism operating with a huge number of concrete notions. At the same time, "primitive thinking" already has abstract concepts. For example, the same drawing placed on different ritual objects means different totemic animals; the same happens with almost identical objects made to denote different animals. However, the abstractions of primitive people differ sharply from the abstract thinking of modern man in one essential element - their mysticism; here we are dealing with a mystical abstraction subordinated to the law of contingency. For instance, there is a certain plant, the harvest of wheat allegedly depends on its ritual gathering; further on, there is also a ritual deer hunting, the harvest of wheat allegedly depends on its quantity. As a result, this very plant ("gikuli"), deer and wheat appear in the consciousness of the tribe as absolutely identical concepts.

Such thinking operation as analogy is not alien to "primitive thinking". For example, if the members of a primitive community (tribe) are divided into a certain number of totems, the same is true for trees, rivers, and stars. A certain tree belongs to such a totem and, therefore, should serve for making weapons, coffins and other objects exactly for people of the given totem.

The language of "primitive thinking" is interesting. One of the distinguishing characteristics of primitive language is its amazing detail and precision in marking objects, situations and actions.

For example, a situation that a modern person would label with the phrase: "A hunter killed a rabbit". An Indian of the North American Ponca tribe would express it as follows: "The man, he alone, alive standing (in imp. case), deliberately killed, by firing an arrow, a rabbit, him, alive, sitting (in vin. case).

The next feature is the absence of the plural. By the example of several languages, L. Levy-Bruhl shows that primitive thinking did not need it. The task of primitive language is to concretize what is seen as much as possible, to convey it with photographic precision and detail; language here is in a sense similar to a photo camera. The meaning of the language of ancient peoples is not abstraction, but linguistic copying (photographing) of these phenomena.

Sign language is also of great importance among ancient peoples. It is very and very rich, actively used by hunters on the hunt, by women during mourning, by witches and herbalists for secret negotiations. There are close links between hand and sound language. "The progress of civilization has as its source the reciprocal action of the hand upon the mind and of the mind upon the hand."

As it has already been mentioned, the language of ancient peoples did not have plurals, and most primitive languages have no designations for numerals more than three. It does not follow that ancient people could not count. Thanks to their phenomenal memory, they could do without numeral names. Instead of numeral names, fingers, wrists and notches are indicated in turn. Consequently, man learned to count long before he had numbers, however paradoxical this conclusion may be, for ancient man never acted independently, but only in a complex set of collective representations and their mysticism. Number has always stood in close connection with the group of objects which it denoted, and hence with their mystical properties. These mystical properties are so strong that even in our society simple numbers (up to about 12) are historically ascribed mystical properties, preserved from those very days.

The analysis of the main activities of primitive people - hunting and fishing - is interesting. When preparing for hunting, only half of the efforts applied goes directly to getting food: making weapons, setting traps, tracking, chasing etc. The second half, often even more important, is directed to establishment of mystical interaction. In order to go hunting, a hunter needs to perform a myriad of magical rituals, which alone can bring him good luck. Before the hunt, dances, incantations and fasts are tied to ensure the presence of game ("bison dance") is performed in order to make the bison appear).

It is necessary to summon the spirit of an animal by means of songs, as it is widely believed that no animal can be killed against its will - it must let itself be killed. The hunter himself, for a few days before the hunt, must fast, abstain from certain words and actions, cleanse himself for better communication with the spirits. The same magic operations are subjected to weapons and hunting equipment, which gives him marksmanship. When the game also depends on mystical rites: it is necessary to negotiate with the horses, to placate the wind and to give strength to the harness. Many rites and incantations for depriving an animal of strength, speed. To complete the hunt it was necessary to placate and thank the spirits, to pacify the killed animals. Any violation of the rituals was fraught with great misfortune, unsuccessful hunting.

Almost the same can be observed in peoples living by fishing. Further, as for the primitive man there is no essential difference between war and hunting, all these rituals also extend on military actions. Rituals similar to them also exist in our society, therefore they are more or less clear to us (different amulets, amulets which people carry with themselves, carry in cars etc.).

However, primitive people have rituals of processes which modern man would not even think of influencing - these are rituals of changing seasons, rain, reproduction of totem animals, growth of young members of the tribe. These rituals are entrusted to a specially dedicated person (priest, shaman, chief, etc.) on whom the life and well-being of the whole tribe depends.

For example, if after the invocation of rain the drought continues, it is attributed to the intrigues of evil spirits, and if the rain begins without performing the ritual, it means that the good spirits themselves, instead of people, performed the ritual.

The king and others continue to interact and care for their tribe even after death, hence the many rituals associated with embalming and other ways of preserving the body after death.

In this way a complex interaction is maintained between the totemic group and its totem, as well as the whole world and all the forces of nature. Sickness is also always some mystical influence, coming either from spirits or from other people. A sick person is a person who has fallen prey to some evil force or bad influence.

For treatment, one turns, of course, to a person capable of communicating with spirits, who must find out exactly what force is harmful here, and banish it. The first thing a healer does is to "prepare" himself for communicating with spirits, here dances, gowns, drums, narcotic substances, etc. come into play. The first reason, which comes to mind of a healer in such altered state of consciousness, is declared to be the cause of the illness. The treatment itself is always deeply mystical.

The same attitude exists to death: it is never natural and is always caused by some deed, violation of customs and influence of evil forces. The law of belonging also applies to the rites of the relation between the living and the dead, when one is not conceived without the other. The dead are honored, spoken to, given presents because their life is fully connected with the life of the living. The spirits of the dead are sometimes considered evil, sometimes good, sometimes they become evil if they are not avenged or something went wrong in the rites. All these rites are deeply mystical, always aimed at establishing a certain connection with higher forces. It is through death that primitive people see the way to discover these connections - all their ceremonies have a moment of ecstasy, "imaginary death", after which there is a "new birth", the discovery of new truths.

It would seem, what significance does "primitive thinking" of long-gone generations have for us - modern people? The matter is that besides purely historical interest, "primitive" forms of thinking are representative in our consciousness in the form of omens and superstitions. The modern man is more mystical than it is considered to be, than we confess it to ourselves. "Periphery" of our consciousness, which is a very significant part of it, is filled with semantic fields carrying information of "primitive thinking". How does this information get into our consciousness? It should be said here that a human being is a recipient of at least three information flows:

1) organized studies or professional;

2) media flow;

3) the flow of domestic communication.

Streams of everyday communication and, partly, mass media are "donors" of individual consciousness of modern man in terms of "pumping" into it all that has been accumulated by mankind at the stage of "primitive thinking" formation. The main form of "primitive thinking" existence today is mysticism, superstition, superstitions and fortune-telling. Speaking of this part of our consciousness, we deliberately separate it from the concept of "folk wisdom", which is represented in the form of proverbs, proverbs, phraseology, etc.

It is worth noting that the main difference between "primitive thinking" and "folk wisdom" is that the latter is a logical positive experience of the development of consciousness, a step forward in the improvement of cognitive activity of mankind. "Folk wisdom" was sensitive to the correspondence of the transmitted experience to the real state of affairs, it taught all the time, suggested how to act, to do in order not to make a mistake, not to repent in the aftermath.

Let's consider in detail what are omens, superstitions, as a modern form of "primitive thinking". Probably, each of us believes in some kind of divination, omens. Millions of people believe and continue to believe in them, regardless of the most categorical taboos on the part of other "reasonable", "reasonable", all-knowing people.

It is difficult and extremely thorny way of the human mind to learn and master the world around us. To obtain any knowledge about nature or themselves, our distant ancestors had to wander for a long time in the jungle of incomprehensible, mysterious, which often seemed miraculous. The word 'superstition' itself means false belief in something (from Old Slavonic 'sue' or 'vece' - in vain, vain). The Dahl dictionary explains superstition as "erroneous, empty, foolish, false belief in something; belief in the miraculous, supernatural, in fortune-telling, divination, omens, signs; belief in cause and effect, where no causal connection is seen".

There are so many superstitions, they are so mixed up and intertwined with each other, with religious ideas and real knowledge, that it is simply impossible to separate them all in a "pure" form and unambiguously classify them, strictly distributing them "on the shelves". It makes sense only conditionally to speak about certain groups of prejudices, for example, domestic, labor, connected with gaps in knowledge of phenomena of surrounding nature, the man himself in social and public processes; numerical, coming from desires to know the future, etc. etc.

It is much more important to understand why sometimes the most naïve (a full bucket of water for good luck, an empty one for bad luck) superstitious beliefs have not died for centuries. Why do they live on in our days, when science more and more often in front of everyone's eyes reveals itself as a powerful force of society? We have to agree, for example, that the reasons of persistence of superstitions and prejudices lie in the peculiarities of our psyche. Certainly, there is another point: many people use superstitious omens without even thinking about it, more often without imagining their mystic essence. Traditions and customs play a major role. Since childhood, faced with various relics of the past, a man gradually gets used to them. It does not even occur to him to think whether it is possible to consider seriously the ancient beliefs. Most often, it concerns domestic superstitions that came "from their grandfathers" and have become almost a habit; they are not perceived as something out of the ordinary. Mystical connections recede into the background here.

There is an omen not to say hello over the threshold. Our ancestors, the ancient Slavs, worshipped the spirits of the dead, believing that they could interfere in their lives, to harm or help the living. People buried their dead under the threshold of the house and tried not to talk near this place: the spirits might offend and quarrel with the guest.

Many of the most ridiculous household beliefs are associated with spirits:

- Your left eye itches, you'll cry,

- the right palm is to receive money.

Where does it come from? In ancient times it was believed that each person is accompanied by two spirits - a guardian angel and a demon - a tempter; the first is near us on the right, the second on the left.

For the same "reason" superstitious people advise to spit three times over the left shoulder to successfully perform the plan. The same ancient remnant we meet: it is impossible to take a ticket in the exam with the left hand - the devil will slip the most difficult one.

What about wishing health to someone who sneezed? The primitive people believed that at that moment, an evil spirit would enter a person's nose. To avoid the danger, you should wish the one who sneezed health.

A man who is used to "consult" everything with omens and beliefs (superstitious man), sometimes he is not satisfied with one or another omen and begins to create these wonderful omens himself in order to ensure his good luck with their help.

If an accidentally broken plate portends happiness, then why not break consciously? The superstitious do so - they break plates "for good luck". If any object "brings good luck", why not keep it with you all the time? So, they hang talismans around their necks.

And if you look at a schoolboy or even a student who believes in omens on the day when he has to pass an exam. When he gets up in the morning, he makes sure not to step on the floor with his left foot, then he looks for the shirt in which he once passed the exam and got a good mark, puts a heel in his shoe and a piece of coloured pencil in his pocket (they say it also helps to get a good mark).

To the above-mentioned beliefs in which the main role is played by evil spirits, the omens associated with religious ideas about the soul are close. A superstition about a broken mirror is widely known. Not knowing laws of light reflection, primitive man could not understand how his reflection appeared in calm water. He believed in the otherworldly world of spirits and believed he saw his double, his soul. Such people began to think that to break it was to kill one's soul, i.e. to kill oneself.

Since ancient times, there has been a belief among people that a horseshoe brings happiness. As a talisman, it was nailed to the door or threshold, so that no misfortune would enter the house. Merchants believed that it could protect goods from thieves, fishermen - to save them from storms.

What is the history of this talisman? A horseshoe, according to the conviction of our ancestors, combines in itself two magic qualities at once.

First, it was made of iron, which evil spirits fear; ancient Romans hammered iron nails into walls of houses to protect themselves from demonic forces. And secondly, the horse belonged to those animals that supposedly helped man ward off hostile spirits. Therefore, in the last centuries above the door or on the roof of many homes strengthened the horse skull, it was later replaced by carved wooden horse head and hooves. This is how the legend of the "lucky horseshoe" came about.

A black cat crossed the road - to be trouble. Thirteen is a fateful number. A mirror broken - to great misfortune. To say hello across a threshold - to quarrel, and also many other things.

Why are people afraid of all this? If you ask someone who turns around when a cat crosses his path, you are unlikely to get any sensible answer. In the best case, he will say that he does so without thinking, out of habit; meanwhile, this widespread superstitious omen is a vivid example of the vitality of the ancient belief, associated with the ideas of our ancestors about the so-called werewolves.

Many people in the past believed that there were witches and devils who liked to turn into cats. And if a man was crossed by the devil himself in a cat's disguise, then, of course, there is nothing to expect for good. Hence comes the expression: "a black cat ran between us. Here, too, it refers to "unclean power", which causes quarrels between people.

Since ancient times black has been a symbol of evil, treachery and frightening uncertainty. It is also the origin of the superstitious notions of the black raven as a sinister bird, and of the night messengers of misfortune - the owl and owl, and of people with unkind black eyes. By the way, from this very association of black with evil comes a belief about the undesirability of meeting with clergymen who wore black vestments.

But let us return to the notorious black cat. It should be noted that this harmless pet has one of the most prominent places in the collection of our superstitious omens. During a thunderstorm, for example, it was recommended to throw a black cat out of a house. Otherwise it would attract lightning. One could not take a cat on horseback - it starts to dry. Even a cat's fur was considered dangerous, as it could cause a toothache.

However, there are not only "cat prophecies", but also other, very common ridiculous household superstitions, superstitions, for example, related to table salt. The most famous of them: to scatter salt is to quarrel. What to do if the salt is already scattered? It turns out that the "misfortune" can help. It is necessary to take a few pinches of salt from the floor and thrice throw over your left shoulder. After all, to the left of us sits the "evil one", which contributed to the fact that the salt would spill.

There are superstitious people who at home and at work, on city streets and away from home constantly see some harbingers of impending events.

A dog will howl in the yard, salt will spill on the table, a mirror will fall and break, three people will light a cigarette from a match, a samovar will hum, etc., etc. - all speaks about something, warns, prophesies.

Let us imagine the life of a man who decided not to ignore a single superstitious omen, not a single divination, not a single prophetic dream, take to heart all the prophecies, strictly follow all the instructions "from above". The life is a torment! Probably that is why the majority of even the most outspoken superstitious people are especially wary of only a few omens - those that touch their being the closest. Among these superstitions are those related to labor activity. Profession, of course, puts its mark on the attitude to the beliefs. If an omen is far from the circle of labor duties, it does not touch a person, and often he simply does not know about it. And having heard about it, he will not take it seriously. The question arises why a city driver needs such an omen: chickens shouting on a roost means a quarrel in the house. The situation is different when it comes to superstitions associated with a black cat, and thus - with the road. Here it can often even explain some related subtleties. It turns out that if a cat runs across the road from left to right and thus does not get "into the floor" of a man's clothes, then nothing yet. It's worse when this "malevolent" animal runs "into the floor" - from right to left. Locomotive drivers know this omen very well. Drivers are also well aware of the belief that a hare has crossed the road. Women with empty buckets are not honored by them either.

During the Great Patriotic War some pilots and tankers tried not to be photographed before the battle. And they willingly did it after the combat mission was accomplished. The same bad omen was considered to be shaving before the fight. A superstitious omen about the left and the right side was also relevant to pilots: to avoid trouble, the glove should be put on the right hand first. The attraction of such superstitions could be explained by the fact that they are associated with professions associated with a certain degree of risk and danger to life. So, to conclude this part, it is necessary to note that "primitive thinking" is the most ancient layer of our consciousness, "languishing" on its periphery. However, from time to time, especially in situations that are logically uncertain, dangerous, stressful, modern man's "cues" of "primitive   is inclined to use thinking".

One form of representation in the consciousness of "primitive thinking" is dreams. "Primitive thinking" is a signified but dologic (pralogical according to Levi-Brühl) form of reflection of the surrounding world, more so inherent to science than to art.

Mysticism and magic are based on the principles of "primitive thinking".

Chapter 5

Manifestation of mystical thinking (magical)

human dreams.

In the second part of this paper we found out that magical thinking of man is a derivative function of the so-called "primitive thinking". Sometimes, however, magical thinking is also partially substantiated from the level of imperative thinking. As a rule, magical thinking is manifested in everyday life of people. Most often, it "suffers" people with poorly developed formal-logical thinking, for example, people poorly educated, poorly studied at school, representatives of Roma nationality, leading up to now an unsettled way of life.

One more form of manifestation of magical thinking in life of a modern man is a dream. However, let us mention that from the point of view of the theory to which I adhere, dreams are most often a consequence of "folding" of magical and imperative thinking. To this day, there is no unified point of view on the nature of dreams in science. Moreover, it is necessary to keep in mind that oneirology (the science of dreams), as well as the modern world psychology consists of different, sometimes mutually exclusive directions.

Oneirology is more of a physiological science than a psychological one, and therefore is more concerned with the physiology of sleep than with its psychology. As we remember from the history of psychology, the first more or less scientific theory of dreams was Freud's psychoanalysis. The point of view I hold in my work is different from the traditional oneurological and psychoanalytic interpretations. Dreaming is a somewhat altered form of mental and conscious existence. The main point of this "alteration" consists in a lowered barrier of energy expenditures, which provides at the moment physiological brain work. Presumably, this is why the "system-science" and "formal-logic" levels of consciousness functioning, as the most energy-consuming ones, work in a saving mode in the dream state; this is why we have sharply reduced criticality of consciousness, if by criticality we mean control of our knowledge from the scientific and formal-logic side. Hence the question arises, if not formal logic, what then cements disparate pictures and images in the dream state, which is the Ariadne's thread of dreams.

It also remains unclear why dreams are so quickly forgotten, despite their personal significance. Presumably, dreams are characterized by a peculiar dissociation of consciousness, as if consciousness works at some lowest initial level. At the same time, images of consciousness (Frege's semantic triangles) enter into various associative connections with the preconscious level of the psyche. This explains the sudden appearance of new information-image blocks during dreams. What is the meaning of such dissociation, what is its psychological mechanism? Practically all authors consider psychological protection as one of the basic tasks of dreams. In modern psychological theories of dreams dedicated to this problem, it is indicated that dreams contribute to the restoration of lost emotional balance. They carry out with the personality, as if a kind of psychotherapy, transferring the passive experiences of the subject with a sense of personal loss, defeat or helplessness to their overcoming, finding a way out, increasing vitality. Other psychological studies have shown that after dreaming, readiness to interact with the unresolved problem is increased, and a sense of competence is restored, which is similar to overcoming feelings of helplessness. It is due to this that the Russian proverb "wiser in the morning" arose.

Here there is another important question that cannot be avoided when analyzing dreams. Does a dream represent a creative act leading to a discovery of something new (the well-known case of D.I. Mendeleev's Periodic Table)? Does this result in search of ways of solution of those real problems that could not be solved in waking, is the search of exit from motivational conflict that during waking led to a state of refusal of search and ousting of unacceptable motive from consciousness performed in a dream? In some cases, all of this actually occurs. However, if we compare the frequency of such discoveries with the fact that many people dream 3 or 4 dreams every night, it becomes obvious that solving creative tasks cannot be considered the main function of dreams.

In this paper, I draw on research that was conducted 20 years ago, over a period of 9 years, during which time over 1500 reports were collected from subjects. Unfortunately, due to the limited possibilities of this work, it is not possible to present the results of this study in a more complete form.

Therefore, I will only cite selectively. Here are some of the dreams I have cited:

- The case of the manager of special projects at the Moscow Youth Palace. This man ended up in hospital with a diagnosis of a double fracture of the spine. After lying there for a week, he saw in one of his dreams a beautiful woman in white. There was a dark void around her. She was spinning in an endless dance. Alexei (that was the manager's name), not for a minute, in his subconsciousness, did not think that this woman could be a prototype, of any medical worker. This dream seemed to be very mediocre and for some reason stuck in his heart. In the morning, quite accidentally, he told it to the nurse on duty. She, in a mundane voice, told him that this is a common situation for them, that all patients who have had this dream (and there turned out to be a lot of them) quickly go to the improvement. Literally 3 days later, the consilium of doctors determined the initial diagnosis of double fracture of the spine - not true. The next day, Alexei was discharged from the hospital.

- Sergey, a military school cadet, 20 years old. He dreams that his friend is wandering around the room. The vision is so vivid that he immediately wakes up and turns on the light in the room. After making sure no one is in the room, he goes back to sleep. The next day, Sergei receives the unpleasant news that his friend has crashed his motorcycle at the very time of the vision.

- Elena Karaseva, 47 years old, planning engineer. Dream: "I see my friend, who is sitting at a big table, at the head of the table, all in white, and on the table a lot of jam of different varieties. I walk up to her and ask: "Valya, what are you doing here? Where is everybody?" And she answers me: "She's sitting and waiting for everyone to come to her wake." I was surprised, knowing in my dream that she wasn't dead, and I left. And she sits and cries. The next day I came to work and found out that Valya had died of a stroke during the night.

- A woman, 35 years old, a speech therapist. "I had a dream that I was walking down the street and fell into a puddle of human excrement. I fall down and start drowning in it. My clothes and body are badly soiled. In real life at the time, I was in a difficult financial situation. A few days after the dream, my husband received a large inheritance.

- Criminal Investigations officer in Moscow. Moscow. About 40 years old. Dream: "I see Kursk railway station during some minor incident. During the situation I have a bag with important documents. But as the dream progresses, all ends well. A week and a half later, in real life, he went to the city of Uglich, on official business. And there he really lost a bag of documents. Two weeks later, Uglich reported the discovery of the bag, and in it, the missing documents.

- Leonidov Nikolay Vasilyevich. Pensioner, 70 years old. Dream of 1976. I dream of a field covered with white snow. A lot of snow, it is clean, fluffy, sparkling in the sun, shimmering. A man was skiing, coming down the ravine. When he wakes up he feels joy and peace of mind. After a while, he gets a big win on a lottery ticket.

Of course, the above list is very insufficient for any conclusions, but this is just as an example. If you try to interpret these dreams, you must first of all pay attention to their mystical nature. The connection of the dream with some future situation. Let us say at once that it is practically impossible to interpret such dreams within the classical psychological paradigm. Therefore, classical psychology does not like explanations of such phenomena. From the point of view of classical psychology, it is all - casual coincidences or game of sick imagination. It would be possible to agree with this, but the fact is that the number of mystical dreams in people, from the point of view of the probability theory, greatly exceeds a certain average statistical norm. The paradigm of the theory of dreams that exists today in psychological science does not allow for the possibility of such foresight of the future, except for random guessing.

One of the variants of the interpretation of a person's "dream behavior" is the theory of anticipation, which was developed by the Soviet psychologist B.F. Lomov [13]. The work of the famous Soviet psychologist V.N. Pushkin on the study of paranormal phenomena, including magical thinking, belongs to the same category of studies of obscure phenomena. [15]

To conclude this chapter, I would like to say that not all mysteries and "strangeness" of our psyche and consciousness are clear to scientists yet, so I am sure that there are a lot of wonderful and interesting discoveries in this field ahead of us.

Chapter 6

Basic principles of the brain to activate its own resources in terms of quantum physics and psychophysiology.

The more we learn about the brain, the more it becomes clear that it is such a complex mechanism that we cannot understand it.

Physiologists have determined the composition of the brain is:

Water 75%

Fat 15%

Protein 7%

The rest are salts, potassium hydrates, etc.

It could be argued that there is nothing more complex in the entire universe than the human brain and its workings. It could be argued that of all the things we know, nothing can be compared to the human brain

Pavlov and these kinds of scientists assume that if we take a bigger magnifying glass or a bigger spectrometer, we will learn more about the nature and workings of the brain, the brain activity. They see the brain as some kind of mechanism, but they have failed to prove this, just as they have failed to prove that the percentage composition of the brain can tell us nothing about how this incredible organism functions.

The brain is a whole world, and it is unlikely that the universe has anything comparable in complexity to the human brain. The number of brain cells, i.e. neurons, is measured in billions, but each neuron has from 10 to 50 thousand connections with other parts of the brain, either with other neurons or with their offshoots. According to some estimates of modern researchers, there are more neurons in the brain than there are elementary particles in the entire Universe, and it is not a question of protein units but of neuron connections.

The amount of information that the human brain can hold is equal to 300 years of continuous viewing of movies, TV shows, etc.

The question is not how much is stored in the brain, but the quality of this information. Information entering the brain is not only what we see, hear, etc., but also how kidneys, liver, etc. work.

That is why it is necessary to train your neural network to live comfortably. Maybe that's why people who do intellectual work and constantly "train" their brain live much longer than others

What is interesting is that the energy expenditure of the brain, i.e. the energy it consumes, is on the order of 10 volts, and in the best moments it can be 30 volts. For example, a supercomputer with much lower performance consumes much more energy, measured sometimes in megawatts.

If we found out how the brain can do with such little power then this information would completely change our Civilization.

If we do a timing experiment, maybe using an evoked potential device, then the brain will show that it made a decision even before you pressed a button or did something like that. You cannot put it down to a motor action, it means that your brain has already made a decision and you do not know about it yet. Moreover, your brain will decide in advance if you make a wrong or right decision.

Limbic system is a set of a number of brain structures. Limbic system is involved in regulation of functions of internal organs, automatic regulation, emotions, memory, sleep, wakefulness, etc.

The limbic system includes:

The hippocampus, is designed to form long-term memory and process and store spatial information.

Almond-shaped body: aggression and caution, fear

Hypothalamus: regulates the autonomic nervous system through hormones, hunger, thirst, sex drive, sleep and waking cycle

The nuchal translucent body for memory formation

Functions of the limbic system:

Receiving information about the external and internal environment of the body, the limbic system triggers autonomic and somatic reactions, which ensure adequate adaptation of the body to the external environment and maintain homeostasis.

Private functions of the limbic system:

- regulation of internal organ function (via hypothalamus);

- formation of motivations, emotions, behavioural reactions;

- plays an important role in learning;

- olfactory function;

- organization of short-term and long-term memory, including spatial memory;

- participation in the formation of orientation and research of the activity -- the organization of a simple motivational and informational communication (speech);

- involvement in sleep mechanisms.

Hypothalamus - regulate neuroendocrine activity of the brain and homeostasis of the body. Research in recent years has shown that the hypothalamus also plays an important role in the regulation of higher functions such as memory and emotional state, and is thus involved in shaping various aspects of behavior.

Hypothalamus controls human endocrine system activity because its neurons are able to secrete neuroendocrine transmitters (liberins and statins) that stimulate or inhibit hormone production by pituitary gland. In other words, the hypothalamus, which mass does not exceed 5% of the brain, is the center of endocrine function regulation; it combines nervous and endocrine regulatory mechanisms into a common neuroendocrine system.

Hypothalamus regulates functions of autonomic nervous system and endocrine system necessary for homeostasis maintenance, participates in organization of behavior required for survival of an organism and a population as a whole in response to changes in internal environment of an organism under various environmental conditions, and is related to such functions as memory, emotions, feeding behavior, reproduction, care of descendants, etc.

Hippocampus is a part of limbic system of the brain (olfactory brain). It participates in the mechanisms of emotion formation, memory consolidation (i.e. transition of short-term memory into long-term memory). The hippocampus retains information while awake and transfers it to the cerebral cortex during sleep. Another function of the hippocampus is to remember and encode the surrounding space (spatial memory), which is why it is activated whenever it is necessary to keep external landmarks that determine the behavior vector in focus.

Basic principles of how the brain works to activate its own resources

The brain directs all of our body's activities.

And so the question may rightly arise, "Who's the boss in the house?", "Who makes the decisions?"

It begs the question, do we have no power over the brain?

And the brain decides everything for us, then you can say, "I'm not responsible for my actions." "It's him, the brain decides everything."

Okay-- I'm doing-- I'm doing great.

It's his fault. It's not my fault.

Some see it as a challenge to our Civilization

It is interesting that there were already trials abroad, when the defendant, really guilty of something, said: "It's not my fault, it's the fault...". However, he called brain - gray matter, not mind - mind

What's my fault if I was born this way? I have a criminal mind!

This shifts our ethical view of the world, calling into question the presumption of innocence.

GB and USA have databases with brain scans of people who have committed various crimes, so they try to make comparisons and identify people prone to various kinds of crimes.

But that can't be an indicator.

The brain sends a signal after you've made a decision, "You made that decision yourself."

So it raises the question of free will

We see and feel that the brain decides what to show us and how.

If there is a glass on the table, everyone sees it differently (quantum physics). The glass is half empty or half full.

If I can't see the glass, it's not there.

Albert Einstein's famous statement "Do you really think the moon only exists when you look at it?"

Literally, Einstein said "I like to believe that the moon is still there even if we don't look at it".

This phrase appeared as a result of a dispute between A. Einstein and Niels Bohr at the Fifth Solvay Congress in 1927. Einstein insisted on preservation in quantum physics of principles of determinism of classical physics (Latin determinate - "to limit, delineate, define" - the doctrine about interrelation and mutual definiteness of all phenomena and processes, doctrine about universal causality) and on interpretation of measurement results from the point of view of "detached observer" (English "detached observer").

On the other hand, Bohr insisted on the fundamentally non-deterministic (statistical) character of quantum phenomena and on the irreducibility of the effect of measurement on the state itself. As the quintessence of these disputes, Einstein's dialogue with Bohr is often cited: "-Bognegerty   .

-Albert ,   don't tell God   what to do ."

And so Einstein's sarcastic question   : "Do you really think the moon only exists when you look at it?"

We can ask ourselves a number of questions:

Am I and my brain the same thing?

Is my identity still there? Or is it not?

And find answers:

We look with our eyes and see with our brains.

We listen with our ears and hear with our brains.

You smell with your nose and the brain gives you the idea of smell.

We can assume that we have the same eyes, but we don't have the same brains. That's even more interesting than differences in fingerprints and corneal irises.

Every brain is unique as it has the neural network of a given personality, a particular life written on it with all the individual associations, what you listened to, what you ate, what you saw.

Every person is strictly individual. In more than ten years of my activity in computer psychodiagnostics I have not met identical individuals. It should be noted that there is a psychology of crowd and the methodology of "Collective intellectual Brain" developed by me, but there it is not the identity of work of the brain and psyche of a person, but about entanglement (from quantum physics) or synchronism ().

The Patriarch of Moscow and All Russia Kirill, discussing the slogan of the French revolution "Liberty, Equality, Fraternity" (Fr. Liberte, Egalite, Fraternite) in the author's program "Word Pastor", expressed his expert opinion, which correlates with the opinion of N.A. Berdyaev, which he expressed in his book "Philosophy of Inequality. Letters to Foes of Social Philosophy", published in Berlin in 1923: "If freedom, there cannot be equality. For freedom is simply a meadow on which flowers and herbs grow, and each herb rises to the measure of its strength. There is no equality: one is stronger, the other is weaker, and the third cannot be seen at all. And if there is equality, it is a mowed lawn, all are equal, but no freedom. If our intellectuals had thought about this earlier, if this comparison had occurred to them, if this comparison had been disseminated in the mass consciousness, they might have been more attentive to this tempting slogan: "Equality, fraternity, freedom", for the revolution was made for freedom in the first place.

It is no exaggeration to say that the only device that can capture and document information recorded in our brain, in our subconscious, is PsyScanner, created using the technique of non-local holographic resonance. PsyScanner reads images that are born after certain neural connections are formed. These are the images that form our behavioral programs, the programs that control not only our behavior, but also our homeostasis, i.e. our life activity.

Homeostasis is a self-regulating process in which all biological systems strive to maintain stability while adapting to certain conditions that are optimal for survival. Any system, being in dynamic equilibrium, seeks to achieve a steady state that resists external factors and stimuli. This statement correlates with one of the basic postulates of quantum physics entropy. This postulate states that in nonequilibrium processes entropy serves as a measure of closeness of the system state to equilibrium, i.e. the greater the entropy, the closer the system is to equilibrium.

Homeostasis is a term used both to describe the existence of organisms in an ecosystem and to describe the successful functioning of cells within an organism. Organisms and populations can maintain homeostasis while maintaining stable levels of fertility and mortality.

In the brain with the help of formed neural connections all information that is received by our brain is recorded. The brain makes a decision after the signal that has passed after all the auditory or visual and other sensory pathways, after that the brain analyzes the signal, I want to clarify that it is not the ear that analyzes the signal, but the brain.

For example: I do not know any Oriental languages. Suppose some text in Arabic or Hindi appears on the screen now, i.e. I can see it with my eyes, but I cannot decode it, because I do not have any key to this text. Because I received this visual signal in my brain and my brain is not prepared to analyze this signal, I am in a hopeless situation, i.e. my vision has worked in vain, I can perceive it as an ornament. It's to the point that it's knowledge that decides. And knowledge is different for everyone.

Therefore, when we look at the same glass we may have fundamentally different associations, the contents of which are directly related to our previous experience based on our learning. The PsyScanner psychodiagnostic and Encoder/ psychocorrection methods are based on this principle.

The first line of the U.S. Declaration of Independence says, "All men are born equal, man is endowed by the creator
inalienable rights".

If we consider the brains of men and women t we see that they are different, the female one is more efficient because it has more gray matter (this is neurophysiological data), then the question arises, "Does it come out that men and women need to be taught differently?"

The second question: "Democracy means that you can go to the Bolshoi Theatre and say 'I will sing for you', to which you will be told 'Do you have the talent and have graduated from the Conservatoire?' Or you go to the Academy of Arts and say 'I want to be a Repin' and you are answered: "Fine, we support you wholeheartedly, but you're not Repin, you don't have the data."

People are not equal, nothing in nature is equal, this may or may not like it, but it is a fact, there are capable and there are not capable, and this is normal and should be accepted

We cannot argue that a person can be born Mozart, Einstein or Perelman.

But you don't have to conclude from that that everyone else has to get into some minor game (minor roles)

In order for children to learn who he is a singer, a trolleybus driver or a scientist a person has to test himself. Schools should not be specialized until a certain point in time.

At some point there will be a division between the able and the very able.

Even though it is written in the U.S. Declaration that everyone is equal, there is a strict selection process. This cannot be offensive, as there are beautiful people and ugly people, tall people and not tall people, etc.

We can say that brain is a non-uniform computer, a part of procedures occurring in brain are similar to computer ones, but there are processes which we can not only repeat but also explain.

For example, wine one likes, another does not, what is the criterion, it is a question of soft, incalculable things, we do not know why if you measure the amount of oil paint put on a canvas by Monet, in no way calculates exactly Monet.

The brain is doing something, and we have no language except the language of art, which is able to describe such things, it describes music, because music is a human language, it describes sculpture, painting, dance. All the arts describe the human from the human.

Now the new iPad generation of Google people is replacing us.

Studies show that the Google generation has a much worse memory than their parents or grandparents.

One English writer: "Before I started living in this virtual electronic world I used to be a wonderful diver (in mental, cognitive sense) I used to dive deep into this ocean of knowledge, I used to swim there for a long time, I used to observe what was passing me by, what was growing there and it absorbed me and I enjoyed it, now I am a surfer, I am hurtling along this ocean at great speed and it never even occurs to me to dive there"

The issue now is the loss of quality, depth, and reliability of knowledge, because people criminally trust unknowingly to whoever wrote the Wikipedia article.

The brain develops all the time, if efforts are made it develops faster than if we make no efforts at all.

When you write by hand, each letter is different, and on the computer all are the same, but on the keyboard they are not arranged in the same way. It's a completely different challenge for the brain. When we write, we are developing fine motor skills, which are in the part of the brain where speech is.

In ancient China, when taking the examinations, people who applied for the posts of high officials submitted two subjects, one of poetry and the other of calligraphy. That's it. That's not what he is and will be there

Human psyche in terms of quantum physics is a non-local reality of our world.

Modern techniques and methods of human mental research cannot fully assess the mental state of a person

We all know very well that widely used test methods practically do not work, no one can say how true the test showed our features, how true this test described our inherent characteristic traits. Test takers widely use a variety of tricks to help get a falsified result. Starting from the fact that in the Internet you can find the right answers, guess what should be the answer, choose the golden mean, and ending with attempts to influence the person who conducts testing. On top of everything else, this diagnosis is very time consuming and the athlete has to spend hours filling out cumbersome tables, the vast majority of tests are translation tests, and therefore often the questions asked are simply not understandable.

Modern psychological tests and polygraph tests are very time consuming and require high professionalism of an employee who conducts them. The results are often directly dependent on the experience and subjective qualities of the specialist, rather than on the personal qualities of the person being tested. Moreover, they have such serious drawbacks as lack of opportunity to determine personal negative qualities, propensity for alcoholism, drug addiction, negative attitude towards management, etc.; high time costs for filling in cumbersome tables; test takers do not always understand the instructions, answer not according to standard; test takers often use distortive tactics, using information from the Internet; no individual approach, the vast majority of test techniques are not valid, that is, reliable, and so on.

We have developed a set of hardware and software tools and techniques that are devoid of the above drawbacks. These hardware-software tools provide invaluable help in solving problems of human reliability analysis, prediction of human behavior and psychocorrection of human behavior.

In the process of scientific research we have developed and implemented tools working on the principle of non-local holographic resonance - PsyScanner psychodiagnostic complex to identify psychological factors affecting the quality of human life and hardware-software complex of computerized psychocorrection Encoder.

Possibilities and working principle of nonlocal holographic resonance are described in Chapter 6 "Nonlocal holographic resonance method and results of its practical application".

The theoretical basis of PsyScanner and Encoder is the theory of non-local holographic resonance based on quantum physics postulates, in particular the phenomenon of "quantum entanglement", as well as on fundamental theoretical concepts of C.G. Jung on the collective unconscious and the phenomenon, defined by Jung as synchronism, on the concept of anticipation created by the Russian psychologist B.F. Lomov, corresponding member of the USSR Academy of Sciences, and on the results of experimental research, which were obtained in Prof. Yung's laboratory.

These studies contrast the principles of quantum physics and Young's synchronicity with the fundamental physical principle of causality and describe synchronicity as an ever-present creative principle in nature that orders events in a "non-physical" (non-causal) way, based only on their meaning, relating to any "non-physical" (non-obvious) relationship between events, regardless of their separation in time and space.

During the experimental research of the PsyScanner methodology we used point information nano impacts on the research object. These point information nano impacts cause phenomena we call non-local holographic resonance, and can be recorded using appropriate PsyScanner tools. With this pointwise influence on the psyche we use PsyScanner's special tools to record the response rate in the process of non-local resonance occurring in the researcher-measurement-procedure-test subject system.

The images embedded in the subject's psyche are synchronized (resonate) with the images embedded in the PsyScanner computer program, i.e. point information micro-interactions on the research object cause the phenomenon of non-local holographic resonance and can be recorded with PsyScanner [10].

Anticipation is anticipation, foreknowledge, perception of an event occurring prior to its perception, anticipation of the event's occurrence. [14]

Anticipation literally means anticipation, i.e. the ability to foresee the development of events, results of actions and phenomena to a certain extent. In terms of time, perception is related to the present, anticipation is related to the future, and memory is related to the past.

Anticipation can be defined as the phenomenon of anticipatory reflection, which can allow "looking into the future". This phenomenon in one way or another relies on the lived experience of each particular person, what happened in the past is preserved in the memory [13].

An example of anticipation can be a feeling of deja vu. Surely each of us has had occasions when we knew in advance what would happen in the next minute or what our interlocutor would do.

In 2015, a group of scientists was awarded the Nobel Prize for the discovery of Grid cells or so-called "coordinate neurons". Grid cells are spatially selective neurons that are a key part of the brain system, building a cognitive map of one's own location in space. These neurons are responsible for the fact that when some events happen to a person, they compare whether such an event has happened in the past and what the individual's reaction was, and, based on this, the person acts according to the same scenario, as if without thinking about it.

An obligatory precondition for the emergence of the phenomenon of anticipation is the preservation of past experience in memory. Thus, if, according to the experience of the past, angina was preceded by, say, discomfort in the throat, then in his subconsciousness an image of ARI or a semantic image of the state of angina arises.

The concept of anticipation implies the response of the semantic core of a particular person's personality to anticipatory reflection, in a broad sense - the body's response and change of its activity with a specific spatial and temporal anticipation in relation to future expected events [14].

Anticipation has a number of functions, such as regulatory, cognitive and communicative. According to Professor B.F. Lomov, the regulative function manifests itself in limitation of the system's freedom levels according to the temporal-spatial structure of the environment. The algorithm of the regulative function consists of preventive preparation, determination of the results and correction of the programme of life processes, as the correction of the regulatory activity necessarily includes the creation of a model of the desired future and comparison of the acquired results of actions with the characteristics of the set end result.

This will condition the direction of development of the situation, which is determined and guaranteed by the process of anticipation because the result will be a future event in relation to the present one. The results of anticipation as anticipation are included in the process of changing the state in one or another direction as necessary and essential components. In this connection the role of the process of anticipation in the regulation of human life activity is very important.

Professor B.F. Lomov believed that "anticipatory reflection" can act in the forms of anticipation (extrapolation, forecasting, anticipation) and goal setting.

Anticipation captures such aspects of situation development as probable variants, transformation of conditions, probable variants of executive acts construction, variants of probable outcomes estimation, probable variants of circumstances model and executive acts program adjustment.

Professor S.G. Gellerstein [5]referred to manifestations of anticipation processes in anticipation of other individuals' actions, which is based on conscious (or not always conscious) knowledge of emotions and the resulting activities.

The principle of PsyScanner is based on non-local holographic resonance which allows identifying even the smallest changes in the semantic state of a person, i.e. is able to catch the slightest changes in the physical and psychological state of a person.

Thus, given the correct psychosemantic resonance program for PsyScanner, we obtain data on the future psychophysiological state of a particular individual.

Hardware-software complex of non-local holographic resonance PsyScanner has been tested and verified for many years in the largest commercial companies such as Vnesheconombank, Rosseti, Tinkoff Bank, Leroy Merlin, etc.

The main advantages of PsyScanner are high reliability (at least 85%); impossibility of falsification of results; no need in special sensors connection; possibility of remote testing via the Internet; possibility of testing unlimited number of people simultaneously; high productivity (a test person answers 2000-2500 questions in 20 minutes); testing protocol is generated as a text.

The main advantages of PsyScanner are the rapid, comprehensive examination via the Internet, as well as a detailed diagnosis report on the symptoms of psychosomatic illnesses.

Chapter 7

Method of nonlocal holographic resonance and results of its practical application

The chapter discusses the non-local holographic resonance method and the results of its practical application.

The method of non-local holographic resonance allows not only to obtain objective information about the psychophysiological state, but also to conduct non-local psychocorrection, which allows more effectively carry out the selection and placement of personnel and provide neutralization of intrapersonal factors of failure and resource disclosure [12].

The principle of non-local holographic resonance method is the following: if some semiotic nano-information is "recorded" on a computer and then presented in a very short time, then psyche of an athlete reacts to such presentation by building a full image. Thus, the use of the method of non-local holographic resonance gives an opportunity to study human psyche, as well as to carry out psychocorrective influence

The devices in question have already been created, have been tested in practice, and have positive results and reviews. The method of psychodiagnostics and psychocorrection is called "nonlocal holographic resonance system", and the devices themselves are called "PsyScanner" holographic psychodiagnostic device and "Encoder" holographic psychocorrection device. All instruments of nonlocal holographic resonance have undergone many years (more than ten years), approbation and verification. The main advantages of these tools created on the basis of non-local holographic resonance are high reliability, ease of use, easy interpretation of the results and very high performance - in 15-20   minutes the test taker answers 2,000 to 2,500 questions.

Thus, we can assert that the principle of holography of human mentality has passed from the theoretical to the practical plane.

In 1637, at the dawn of Cartesian science in Leiden, a work by René Descartes, then still little-known author and later founder of a new science based not only on introspection, but also on experiment, was published. It was called "Discourse on the method for the right direction of reason and the search for truth in the sciences".

In this book Descartes first formulates his most famous statement, "I think, therefore I exist," as well as outlining four basic rules of cognition:

1. to consider only what is obvious to be true;
2. divide each problem into its component parts;
3. to reason from the simple to the complex;
4. regular inventories and reviews [6].

The rules of cognition formulated by Descartes determined the vector of classical science for centuries to come. Based on Descartes' reasoning, another great founder of empirical science, John Locke, put forward the idea of "psychological atomism". Based precisely on "psychological atomism," as early as the end of the 19th century (December 1879) Wilhelm Wundt creates in Leipzig the first laboratory of experimental research in the history of psychology.

Emerged after 1890, in Francis Galton's school, the first methods of purely psychological study - tests - were based on the elementary principle: to understand something, including the psyche, it must first be divided into elementary parts.

Several levels of understanding of the "whole" have developed in the history of science.

First level. The whole is understood as a certain group of elements arranged together in a certain area, as a sum of some units.

The second level of understanding of the whole is a system of a more complex order. There are elements in it, connections between the elements are tighter than connections of the elements with the "outside" world.

The third level integrity is related to the fact that the elements included in the system acquire radically different qualities than before they entered it.

The fourth level of integrity development is the situation when the elements exist only in the system, forming a kind of universal device, which does not arise by itself, but only when certain conditions are met.

At the highest fifth level of integrity there is a situation when integrity exists but the elements that should be part of it are absent. If we speak about the material world, such phenomena occur in holograms.

Non-local holographic resonance

A hologram is an integrity not consisting of primary elements. Both physical holograms and mental image are constructed as non-localized in structural relation phenomena. Any point of a holographic medium (plate) contains a complete set of information about the whole. But this is from a purely spatial point of view, but if we try to consider a hologram from a temporal point of view we will discover no less interesting properties [10].

For example, a mental image is a hologram, which contains a certain set of information about an object, and all information can be recorded in two-dimensional space.

If this information, from a two-dimensional medium, is presented "partially", in a very short time interval, then psyche, building the volumetric form (three-dimensional) will still restore the whole by any tiny spatial or temporal component [11].

For example, if we "record" some information (figurative or semiotic) on a computer and then present it to a person within a short period of time, it appears that this presentation causes a person's psyche to react to it by forming a complete image, which may be confirmed by certain motor reactions of the person.

Thus, a person's psyche can be studied, corrected, and helped to get rid of unnecessary habits, etc. We called this method of psychodiagnostics and psychocorrection   "the system of nonlocal holographic resonance"

The theoretical basis of the principle of operation of these tools and techniques is based on basic provisions of quantum physics, such as holography, i.e. the ability to preserve and restore the integrity of the human "self" and its accumulated information and the phenomenon of "quantum entanglement", a special case of which can be considered as Young's synchronism. [17, 18]

When organizing our own experimental investigations of our methodology we used point information nano-micro-actions on the research object. These point informational nano-micro impacts cause the phenomena called by us as non-local holographic resonance, reconstruct a holistic picture, which can be recorded by means of corresponding instruments.

As a result of studies of non-locality of human psyche we came to a conclusion that an important condition of appearance of holographic resonance is the phenomenon of amplification of signals coming from human subliminal sensations.

In practical research using the PsyScanner technique we have used point information nano micro-exposures on the research object. These point impacts are recorded using PsyScanner toolkit, which determines the rate of response to subthreshold images in the process of nonlocal holographic resonance, that occurs in the researcher-test subject system.   measurement procedure
In the process of research, the images embedded in the psyche resonate with the images embedded in the computer program and cause the phenomenon of non-local holographic resonance, which is recorded with PsyScanner [10, 11, 12].

As already mentioned, PsyScanner and Encoder are hardware-software - complexes that have been used in the selection and training of highly qualified athletes both in Russia and abroad for more than ten years [10].

We all know very well that widely used test methods practically do not work, no one can say how true the test showed our features, how true this test described our inherent characteristic traits. Test takers widely use a variety of tricks to help get a falsified result. Starting from the fact that in the Internet you can find the right answers, guess what should be the answer, choose the golden mean, and ending with attempts to influence the person who conducts testing. Apart from everything else, this diagnostics is very time-consuming and the athlete has to fill in cumbersome tables for hours, the vast majority of tests are translation ones, and therefore often asked questions are simply not understandable [11].

Within the framework of our research work, together with the Moscow University of the Ministry of Internal Affairs and the Expert-Criminalistics Center of the Ministry of Internal Affairs of the Russian Federation, we carried out studies comparing data obtained using polygraph examination and non-local holographic resonance method (PsyScanner). The results were fully correlated, and the time costs were not comparable: Polygraph - 2.5 - 3 hours, PsyScanner - 8 - 10 minutes [2].

Modern psychoanalysis is too time-consuming: It requires a fairly large number of meetings to consult with a psychoanalyst. The great traumatic nature of the identified experiences cannot be overlooked.

During PsyScanner testing, using non-local holographic resonance for a few minutes, we identify and document indicators such as:
- propensity to use alcohol
- drug abuse
- Theft
- family issues
- knowingly leaking confidential information for money
- deliberate management fraud
- personal motivations fear, money, careerism
- Being result-oriented and demonstrating initiative in the work process
- and much more on the customer's request

In today's widespread psychotherapeutic approaches and schools, for all their variety, there is something that unites them - the necessity of contact between the psychologist and the client. Until contact is established, the psychologist can neither make a diagnosis, nor can he or she reasonably select the type of psychological approach or relate his or her internal experience to the internal experience of the client. In other words, psychotherapy requires contact - contact provides understanding - understanding determines success in identifying positive and negative qualities of employees.

When the basic theme is the identification of components, for example, traumatic experiences from negative experiences with the management or identified cases of negative actions, such contact can be painful, frightening in its severity and the employee may avoid deep productive contact with the psychologist. Often defaults, absolutely stereotyped turns, ready formulas (all is well, all is bad, sayings, clichés, etc.) are used for this purpose. Sometimes complete defaults are framed as one-word answers. And often on the contrary, as the strategy is chosen the story, which is connected with real events only indirectly: real events are intertwined with stories of other people, with own fantasies. Thus, instead of comprehending real inner experience, a "frozen narrative" emerges.

Advantages of non-local holographic resonance method over other methods

The advantage of the non-local holographic resonance method is that there is no need for contact between the psychologist and the person being tested. This eliminates the possibility of such distortions. The psychologist, there is no need to conduct questioning, to "get into the soul", to force recall and analyze unpleasant traumatic experiences. As experience shows, the classical methods and techniques of psychoanalysis used in work with ordinary people fit poorly into the complex mechanism of working with highly qualified employees. Apparently this is why many key employees, having tried it once, do not want to work with psychologists.

The main advantages of non-local holographic resonance over other methods and techniques are its high performance. The subject is asked about 2,500 questions in 20 to 25 minutes, to which he/she answers truthfully at the subconscious level. As a result, hidden and hidden in the subconscious information reveals the true motivation of actions, intentions, and reasons for behavior. In order to obtain such volume and quality of information, the psychologist usually needs more than half a year of time. By this time, the information obtained undoubtedly becomes outdated.

Based on the above, we can state that the method of non-local holographic resonance is aimed at activation and increase of internal capabilities of the organism, stress resistance, elimination of psycho-emotional tension ,
optimization of
psycho-emotional state, gaining self-confidence, overcoming fear, inner anxiety and other negative states, as well as overcoming psychosocial problems.

Examples of practical applications of nonlocal holographic resonance

1. The first experience of working with highly qualified athletes was received in December 2003 - January 2004. - Department of Athletics of the Russian State University of Physical Culture and Sport, the work was carried out during 1 month. The results obtained: women and men (qualification of Master of Sports) running 200 m - 0.49 sec (mean result 23 - 24 sec), 300 m - 0.56 to 0.69 sec (38 - 39 seconds), 400 m - 0.7 to 0.6 sec (47 seconds). In the informational letter on the results of the work done by the head of the Department of Theory and Methodology of Track and Field Athletics Candidate of Pedagogical Sciences Arakelyan and Honored coach of Russian Federation Assistant Professor Trefilov made the following   conclusion
research, which is especially relevant in the run-up to the Olympic Games".

2. In May-August 2008 on the instruction of Russian Federation State Committee for Sports training to Olympic Games fencers E. Lamonova and A. Frosin were conducted, the result of the work was that E. Lamonova became the

Olympic champion.

3. In August 2009-February 2010 the Russian sprint cross-country skiing team was trained. In the letter of thanks from the Chairman of the Russian Cross-Country Skiing Federation, gratitude was expressed for the training of athletes who achieved the following results Kryukov - gold medal, Panzhinsky - silver medal, Petukhov and Morilov - bronze medal, Devyatyarov - 8th place, Korostyleva and Khazova - bronze medal

4. From May 2010 to February 2017, successful work on the preparation of the sprint team of the Russian Federation was carried out, which was noted in the Letter of Gratitude of the FLGR. Achieved results: N.Kryukov - three-time World Champion, silver medalist of the 2014 Olympics, multiple champion of the World Cup stages. A.Petukhov - World Champion, silver medallist of the World Championship, multiple winner of stages of the World Cup. N.Morilov, multiple winner of stages of the World Cup. N.Matveeva is silver medallist of the World Championship, multiple winner of the World Cup stages.

5. In May 2021, psychological testing was conducted on a large organization as part of a tender for a very large government contract. The results revealed: personal enrichment (bribes) - 34%, drugs - 35%, psychological burnout - 29%, gaming - 36%, consciously leaking information for money - 30%, etc. The management decided to rotate employees.

7. Since December 2020, recruitment and existing employees of LeroyMerlin's network of stores (over 130) are regularly screened.

Conclusion and findings

Thus, in conclusion we can state the following. The psyche is a complex multilevel formation. Of course, the central link in the development of the psyche is consciousness as a sign system of mental reflection. The system-forming factor of multilevel consciousness is a complex combination of mystical and formal-logical thinking. The levels that emerged in phylogenesis are equally inherent in modern humans. In developing, the psyche and consciousness pass through all phylogenetic stages of development during ontogenesis. That is why modern man has mystic-magic thinking inherited from his primitive ancestor. Unfortunately, modern methods of psychodiagnostics are oriented mainly on the study of the formal logical layer of consciousness, completely overlooking "primitive thinking". This leads to a one-sided view of the development of the human psyche and the organization of human activity. The task of modern psychology is to develop methods that actively study all levels of consciousness and psyche.

Thus, we can assert that the principle of human psyche holography is moving from the theoretical plane to the practical one in many fields of human activity. Using the toolkit of non-local holographic resonance will make personnel selection and placement more effective and provide neutralization of intrapersonal factors of failure and unlock resources for high achievements in all types of human activity

Bibliography:

1. Aristotle On the Soul / Aristotle ; [translated from Greek by P.S. Popov; footnote by A.V. Sagadeev;

2. Act of introduction in scientific activities of the Moscow University of the Ministry of Internal Affairs of Russia named after V.Y. Kikotya on 26 May 2021.

3. Wundt W. Introduction to Psychology. St. Petersburg: Peter, 2002. - 32.

4. Vygotsky. Thinking and Speech. Ed. 5, revised. - Publishers Labyrinth, M., 1999. - 172 c.

5. Gellerstein S.G. Psychotechnics. Moscow: Novaya Moskva, 1926. 239 c.

6. Descartes Renee Publisher: Eksmo-Press, 2015. , ISBN: 978-5-699-82972-9, P/ 128

7. Levy-Bruhl. Lucien The supernatural in primitive thinking. MOSCOW, 1999, P.338.

8. Lyzova. - M. : RIPOL Classic, 2020. - 260c. - (PSYCHE).

9. Leibniz New Experiments on the Human Mind. MOSCOW - L., 1936. C.106.

10. Lebedev I.B., Kuznetsov A.Y. Metodologicheskiye osnovy formirovaniya programnykh diagnosticheskikh kompleks // Psikhologiya. Historico-critical - reviews and modern research. 2019. T. 8. № 6A. C. 286-291. DOI: 10.34670/ AR.2020.46.6.181].

11. Lebedev I.B., Kuznetsov A.Y. Innovative approaches to psychodiagnostics and personality psychocorrection at the present stage // Psychology. Historical and critical reviews and contemporary research. 2019. T. 8. № 6A. C. 277-281. DOI: 10.34670/AR.2020.46.6.182

12. Lebedev I.B., Kuznetsov A.Yu. Psyche as a nonlocal reality of our world // Psychology. Historical-critical reviews and contemporary research. 2019. T. 8. № 6A. C. 295-300. DOI: 10.34670/AR.2020.46.6.184

13. Boris Fedorovich Lomov. Anticipation in the structure of activity ; Moscow: - Science 1980.

14. Lomov B.F., Belyaeva A.V., Nosulenko V.N. Verbal encoding in cognitive processes of analysis of auditory image features. Moscow: Nauka, 1986. 128 c.

15. Pushkin V.N., Dubrov A.P. Parapsychology and modern natural science ; M.: Sovaminko 1989. - 280c.

16. Smirnov I., Beznosyuk E., Zhuravlev A. Psychotechnologies. Computer psychosemantic analysis and psychocorrection at the unconscious level. Moscow: Progress, 1995.

17. Jung K.G. Synchronicity: the akausal unifying principle // K.G. Jung. Synchronicity. Moscow: Reflebuk, 1997. 7. Niebur E. Saliency map // Scholarpedia. 2007. No. 8(2). URL:

18. Pauli W. The Interpretation of Nature and the Psyche. New York: Pantheon Books, 1955.

19. Tsuchiya N., Koch C. Attention and consciousness // Scholarpedia. 2008. No. 5(3). URL:

20. Goferman S., Zelnik-Manor L. Context-aware saliency detection // IEEE Trans. Pattern Analysis and Machine Intelligence. 2012. P. 1915-1926.

21. Pribram, Karl H. // The Corsini Encyclopedia of Psychology and Behavioral Science Volume 3 / W. Edward Craighead (Editor), Charles B. Nemeroff (Editor). - Third Edition. - Wiley, 2002. - — P. 1241. - — 1952 p. - ISBN 978-0-471-27082-9

22. Tsuchiya N., Koch C. Attention and consciousness // Scholarpedia. 2008. No. 5(3). URL:

Printed by Books on Demand GmbH, Norderstedt / Germany